CRAFTS FOR ALL SEASONS

CREATING WITH
SALT DOUGH

Important Note to Children, Parents, and Teachers
Recommended for children ages 9 and up.
Some projects in this book require cutting, painting, baking, gluing, and the use of small materials. Young children should be supervised by an adult. Due to differing conditions, individual levels of skill, and varying tools, the publisher cannot be responsible for any injuries, losses, or other damages that may result from use of the information in this book.

Published by Blackbirch Press, Inc.
260 Amity Road
Woodbridge, CT 06525

©2000 by Blackbirch Press, Inc.
First Edition

Original Title: *Modela con pasta de sal* by Anna Llimós and Laia Sadurní; photography by Nos y Soto; illustration by Núria Giralt
Original Copyright: ©1996 Parramón Ediciones, S.A., World Rights, Published by Parramón Ediciones, S.A., Barcelona, Spain.

e-mail: staff@blackbirch.com
Web site: www.blackbirch.com

Printed in Spain

10 9 8 7 6 5 4 3 2 1

Library of Congress Cataloging-in-Publication Data
Llimós, Anna.
[Pasta de sal. English]
Creating with salt dough / by Anna Llimós and Laia Sadurní.
  p. cm. — (Crafts for all seasons)
Includes bibliographical references and index.
Summary: Provides instructions for using dough to create a variety of craft projects, including a snake bookmark, napkin rings, a hair-clip worm, ladybug belt, picture frame and more.
ISBN 1-56711-435-0
1. Bread dough craft—Juvenile literature. [1. Bread dough craft. 2. Handicraft.]
I. Sadurní, Laia. II. Title III. Series: Crafts for all seasons (Woodbridge, Conn.)
TT880.L63413 2000
745.5—dc21
98-38942
CIP
AC

Contents

Adult supervision is strongly recommended.
The crafts in this book involve baking.

CRAFTS FOR ALL SEASONS

CREATING WITH
SALT DOUGH

B L A C K B I R C H   P R E S S ,   I N C .
WOODBRIDGE, CONNECTICUT

Crab Cap

1. Flatten a ball of dough and cut a line in the center.

☛ **YOU'LL NEED: dough (see page 30), paints, varnish, glue (optional), a jar with a cap.**

2. Attach two small balls for eyes and six rolls for legs.

3. For the claws, form a roll and split it halfway, as shown. Make another roll just like it.

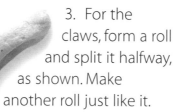

4. Attach the claws and add crab markings.

5. Bake the crab and paint it after it cools. When it is completely dry, you can varnish it.

6. Glue the crab to the cover of a glass jar and fill it with candy.

7. You can also make a sly little mouse trying to get at the cheese inside the jar.

💡 **Use your imagination:**
Try making some other crusty creatures the same way—make a lobster or other kinds of crabs.

Charmed Snake Bookmark

☞ YOU'LL NEED: dough, a rolling pin, markers, and construction paper or colored ribbon.

1. Flatten a ball of dough with a rolling pin.

2. Form it into a basket shape.

3. Roll several pairs of long strips and braid each pair.

4. Attach the braids to the basket base. Place the thicker braids on the upper part. Don't forget the handles.

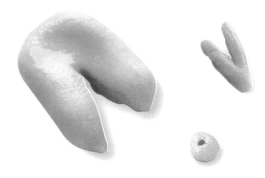

5. For the snake's head, flatten a small ball of dough and split it partway. Attach a tongue to the inside of the mouth and an eye to the upper part of the head.

6. Bake the head and the basket. After they've dried and cooled, paint the head and varnish the basket.

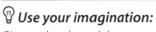

7. To connect the head and the basket, cut a wavy strip of ribbon or construction paper and color it with markers.

💡 *Use your imagination:*
Since a bookmark has two ends, you can make them out of related items, like toast and a toaster or an Eskimo and an igloo. What other pairs can you think of?

A Salty Sea Aquarium

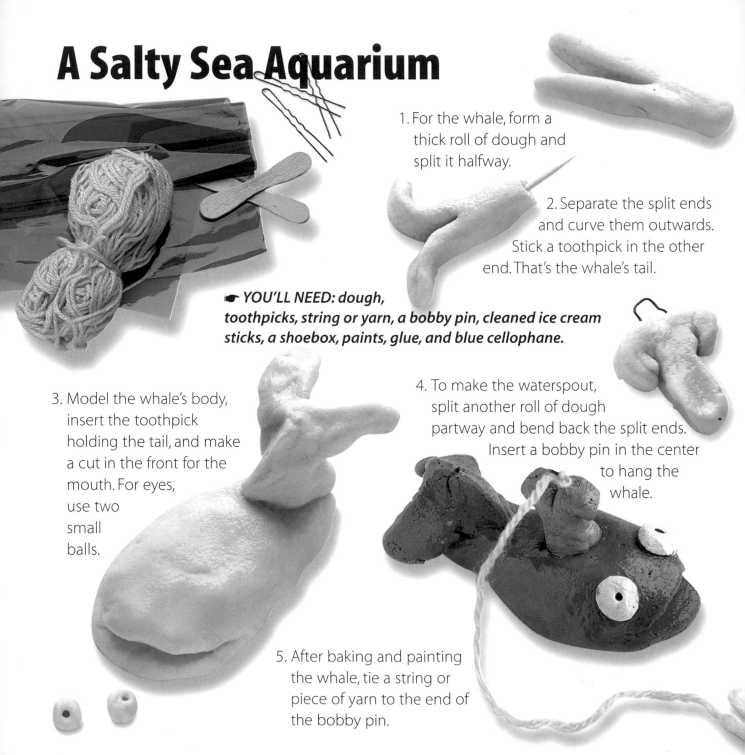

1. For the whale, form a thick roll of dough and split it halfway.

2. Separate the split ends and curve them outwards. Stick a toothpick in the other end. That's the whale's tail.

☛ **YOU'LL NEED: dough, toothpicks, string or yarn, a bobby pin, cleaned ice cream sticks, a shoebox, paints, glue, and blue cellophane.**

3. Model the whale's body, insert the toothpick holding the tail, and make a cut in the front for the mouth. For eyes, use two small balls.

4. To make the waterspout, split another roll of dough partway and bend back the split ends. Insert a bobby pin in the center to hang the whale.

5. After baking and painting the whale, tie a string or piece of yarn to the end of the bobby pin.

6. Find a shoe box, cut a rectangular opening in one of the long sides, and decorate it like an aquarium. Attach a piece of blue cellophane to the front to look like water.

7. Make other sea creatures in the same way. Hang them from an ice-cream or other small stick.

8. Place your fish inside the aquarium, and you'll have a bit of the salty sea in your very own room!

💡 **Use your imagination:** *Create other sea creatures to put in your aquarium – try sea stars, shells, and an octopus made from a ball and eight rolls!*

Worm to Wear

☞ **YOU'LL NEED: dough, a hair clip, a toothpick, a butter knife, paint, construction paper (optional), and glue.**

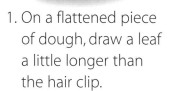

1. On a flattened piece of dough, draw a leaf a little longer than the hair clip.

2. Shape a roll of dough for the worm.

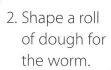

3. Cut out the leaf and place the worm on top of it.

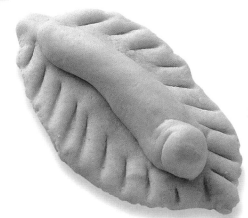

4. Use two little balls of dough for the eyes. With a toothpick, draw the worm's mouth and rings.

5. Bake the piece, then paint it and glue it to the hair clip. For a stronger hold, glue construction paper to your clip first, then glue your worm to the paper.

Cat Clip

☞ YOU'LL NEED: dough, a rolling pin, a butter knife, a hair clip, paint, glue, and construction paper (optional).

1. Roll out a piece of dough.

2. Draw and cut out the body and paws of a cat seen from the front.

4. Join the head to the rest of the body; add eyes and nose. Mark the whiskers and place the piece in the oven.

5. You can paint the cat and glue it to the clip. For a stronger hold, cut a piece of construction paper and glue it between the clip and the cat.

3. On a smaller piece of flattened dough, draw and cut out the cat's head.

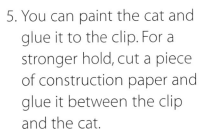

6. You can also make a fish, a bird, a coiled snake, or whatever else your imagination comes up with!

Lovable Gnomes

☞ *YOU'LL NEED: dough,*
toothpicks, bottle caps, candles,
cardboard, and paint.

1. To make a gnome's body, form a thick roll of dough and cut off a piece.

2. Make the arms and the legs out of a thinner roll cut into four pieces.

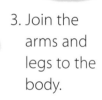

3. Join the arms and legs to the body.

4. Use a ball of dough for the head and secure it to the center of the body with a toothpick.

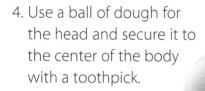

5. Mold the cap in the shape of a pyramid with a bent tip.

6. For the cakes, flatten several balls of dough and use different size bottle caps to mark circles in them.

7. Use a toothpick to mark a border on the largest circle.

9. Place the circles on top of each other, from largest to smallest. Bake and paint the gnomes and the cake (take the candles out first).

8. Make a hole for the birthday candle in the center of the smallest circle.

10. Place the figures on a circle of construction paper glued to a circle of cardboard or cork.

All you need now are a few more candles and you can decorate your own birthday cake!

💡 **Use your imagination:** *You can turn these figures into elves for really great Christmas ornaments! Just add little beards, and attach small balls to the ends of their hats. You can also stick half a paper clip in their tops before baking, so you can hang them by a string.*

13

Neat Napkin Rings

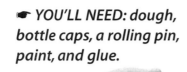

☞ YOU'LL NEED: dough, bottle caps, a rolling pin, paint, and glue.

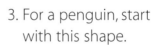

1. For a fish or snake ring, roll a long, thick strip of dough.

2. Bend it over as shown in the photo and attach the eyes according to the animal you're making.

3. For a penguin, start with this shape.

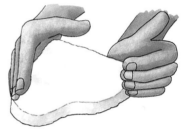

4. Use a bottle cap or film container to cut out the stomach.

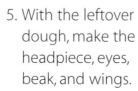

5. With the leftover dough, make the headpiece, eyes, beak, and wings.

6. For a ladybug, flatten a piece of dough with a rolling pin and shape it into a rectangle.

7. Join the ends of the rectangle to form a ring.

8. Flatten another piece of dough and draw on it a leaf with its veins.

9. Use a small ball of dough for the ladybug's head and a larger one for its body. Bake the pieces separately, let them cool, then paint and glue them together.

10. Now get your napkins and set the table in style!

💡 **Use your imagination:** *Using a circle shape as your center, what other shapes and animals can you make? How about an inchworm, a vine of ivy, or some "pretzels"?*

15

A Snazzy Starship

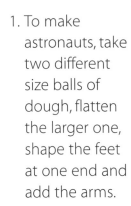

☞ **YOU'LL NEED:**
*dough, bobby pins,
butter knife, modeling
clay, aluminum foil,
paints, glue, cardboard,
scissors, and string.*

1. To make astronauts, take two different size balls of dough, flatten the larger one, shape the feet at one end and add the arms.

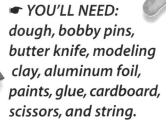

2. Join the head and the body, add a breathing mask, and mark the eyes.

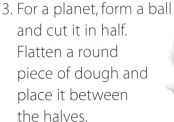

3. For a planet, form a ball and cut it in half. Flatten a round piece of dough and place it between the halves.

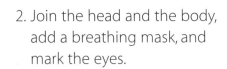

4. For stars, flatten a ball of dough and cut out a star shape.

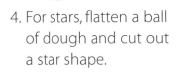

5. Make any other figures you can think of. Don't forget to insert the end of a bobby pin at the top of each one. Have an adult cut the bobby pin for you with a wire cutter.

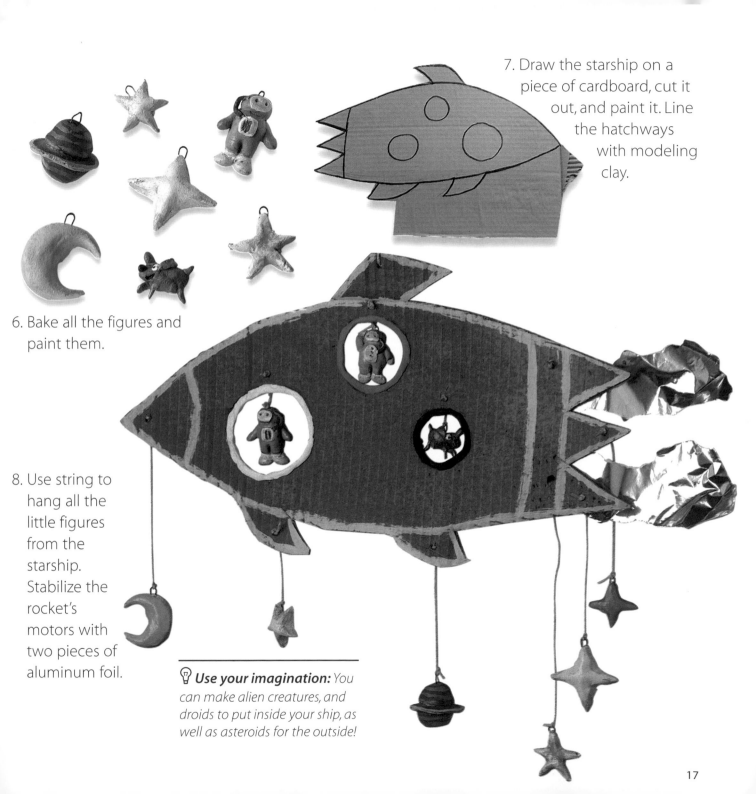

7. Draw the starship on a piece of cardboard, cut it out, and paint it. Line the hatchways with modeling clay.

6. Bake all the figures and paint them.

8. Use string to hang all the little figures from the starship. Stabilize the rocket's motors with two pieces of aluminum foil.

💡 **Use your imagination:** *You can make alien creatures, and droids to put inside your ship, as well as asteroids for the outside!*

17

Little Devil Candle Holders

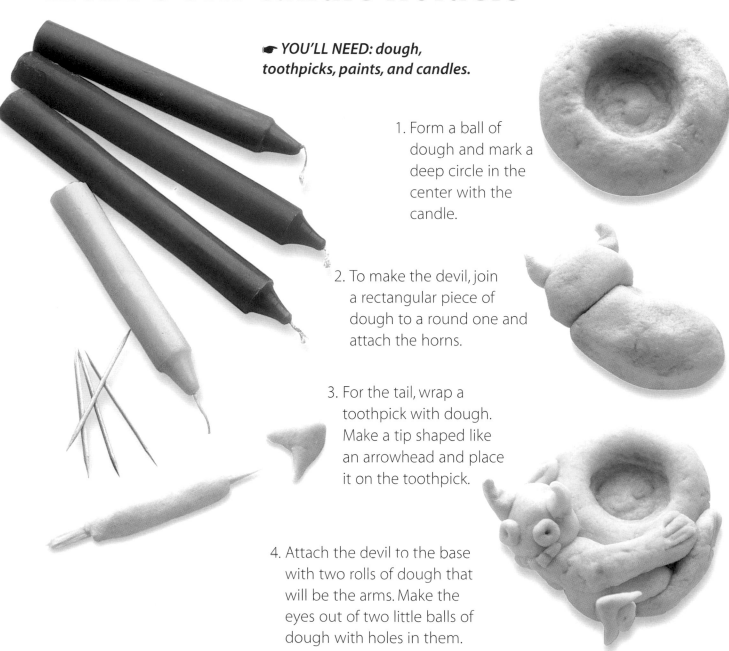

☛ *YOU'LL NEED: dough, toothpicks, paints, and candles.*

1. Form a ball of dough and mark a deep circle in the center with the candle.

2. To make the devil, join a rectangular piece of dough to a round one and attach the horns.

3. For the tail, wrap a toothpick with dough. Make a tip shaped like an arrowhead and place it on the toothpick.

4. Attach the devil to the base with two rolls of dough that will be the arms. Make the eyes out of two little balls of dough with holes in them.

5. Bake the piece, let it cool, then paint it.

6. Your candle holder is ready. All you need now is a candle in the center!

💡 *Use your imagination:*
You can also make something a bit wetter, like this frog. Or, you can make shapes and colorful designs as your base!

Ladybug Belt

☞ **YOU'LL NEED: dough, wire, a belt, paints, varnish (optional).**

1. Roll out a thick strip of dough.

2. Join the two ends to make a circle. Attach a ball for the head and several little balls for spots.

3. Use two little balls of dough for the eyes and two more, each attached to a piece of wire, for the antennae.

4. Join all the parts and bake them.

5. Let the ladybug cool, then paint it.

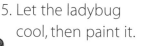

6. Place the ladybug on a belt and see what a cool buckle it makes! You could also put it through the straps of your bookbag or knapsack!

Magnet Magic

☛ **YOU'LL NEED: dough, blunt knife, rolling pin, caps, paints, and small, flat magnets.**

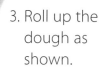

1. Roll out dough with a rolling pin or a cylindrical container.

2. Use a blunt-edged knife to cut out a triangle.

3. Roll up the dough as shown.

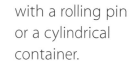

4. Form two little balls, flatten them a little, and make a small hole in each center. These will be the eyes.

5. Bend the ends of the croissant and attach the eyes. It's now ready to bake.

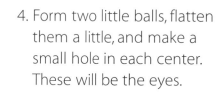

💡 **Use your imagination:** *Make other foods, like bananas, grapes, asparagus, or this fun carrot. After the paint or varnish dries, glue a magnet to the back.*

6. You can paint this piece, but its color will be much more real if you only use varnish. When it is completely dry, glue a magnet to the back.

A Submarine Snapshot Frame

☞ YOU'LL NEED: *dough, a round cap, thick board or the back of an old notebook, bobby pins, toothpick, photos, paints, glue, and a rolling pin.*

1. Use a rolling pin to roll out a dough surface large enough for your frame, then shape it into an oval.

2. With a round bottle cap, mark and cut out holes for the four windows.

3. Roll a long thin strip and attach it to the edge of the oval. Line the windows with strips of dough; use a toothpick to mark little lines on them.

4. For the propeller, join two rolls of dough with a little ball. Mark a line down the center.

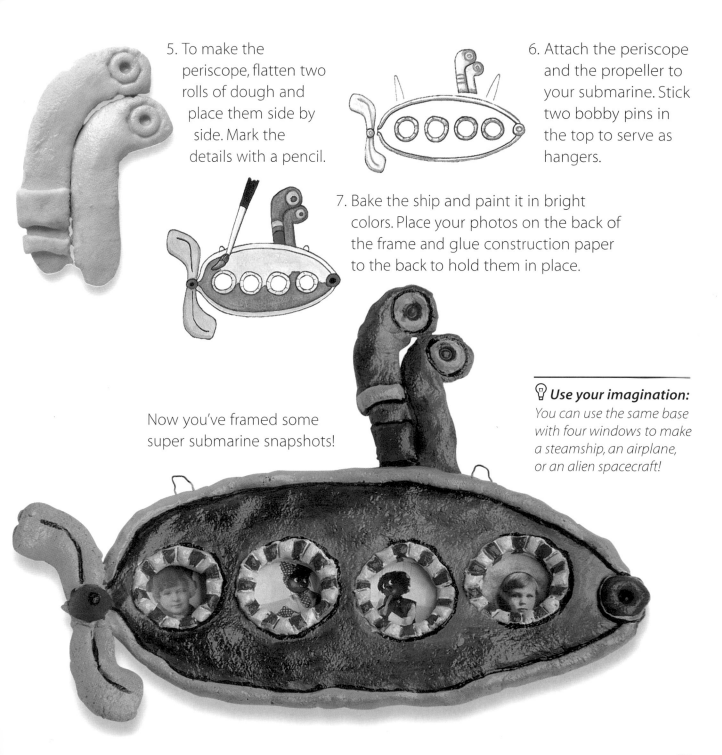

5. To make the periscope, flatten two rolls of dough and place them side by side. Mark the details with a pencil.

6. Attach the periscope and the propeller to your submarine. Stick two bobby pins in the top to serve as hangers.

7. Bake the ship and paint it in bright colors. Place your photos on the back of the frame and glue construction paper to the back to hold them in place.

Now you've framed some super submarine snapshots!

💡 **Use your imagination:** *You can use the same base with four windows to make a steamship, an airplane, or an alien spacecraft!*

Helpful Hippoclip

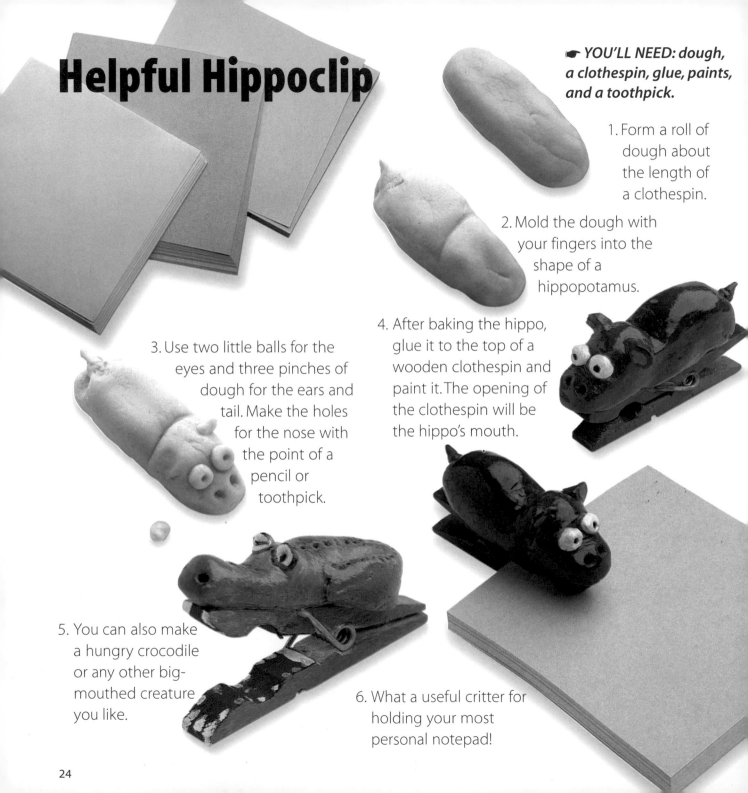

☛ **YOU'LL NEED: dough, a clothespin, glue, paints, and a toothpick.**

1. Form a roll of dough about the length of a clothespin.

2. Mold the dough with your fingers into the shape of a hippopotamus.

3. Use two little balls for the eyes and three pinches of dough for the ears and tail. Make the holes for the nose with the point of a pencil or toothpick.

4. After baking the hippo, glue it to the top of a wooden clothespin and paint it. The opening of the clothespin will be the hippo's mouth.

5. You can also make a hungry crocodile or any other big-mouthed creature you like.

6. What a useful critter for holding your most personal notepad!

Placecard Clowns

1. Roll out a piece of dough and make two cuts in the top.

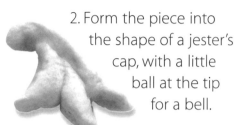

2. Form the piece into the shape of a jester's cap, with a little ball at the tip for a bell.

3. To make the face, flatten a ball of dough and mark the mouth and eyes.

4. Fold a long strip of dough like an accordion and use it to make clown-costume collars.

☞ **YOU'LL NEED: dough, clothespins, paints, and glue.**

5. Join all the parts together and place them in the oven. Let them cool, then glue the clown to a colored or painted clothespin.

6. When you have a party, use these clips to hold placecards with your guests' names written on them!

Key Kritters

☞ YOU'LL NEED:
dough, cap or round containers, bobby pins, paper clips, paint, and a key ring.

1. Form a ball of dough, flatten it, and mark a circle with a small film container.

2. Remove the circle from the rest of the dough and repeat these steps. The circles will be the elephant's ears.

3. Place the ears on a larger circle, which will be the body, and add a roll of dough for the trunk.

4. Make the four legs and the tail out of little rolls of dough. Mark the eyes and other details. Stick a paper clip or bobby pin into the rear side of the elephant's back.

5. Place it in the oven, let it cool, then paint it. Hook a key ring to the clip and there's your key elephant!

💡 **Use your imagination:** *Make a whole zoo full of keyring beasts, like pigs, snakes, birds, mice, or this octopus!*

"Baa-Baa Black Sheep" Mobile

☛ **YOU'LL NEED: dough; bobby pins; wide, colored ribbons; cotton; glue; and paints.**

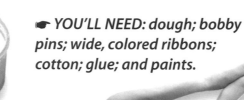

1. To make the wreath, roll two long strips of dough and braid them.

2. Join the ends of the braid to form a circle. Repeat these steps to make a smaller circle.

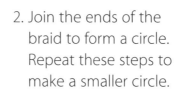

3. For each sheep, join two pieces of dough and model the body and head. Stick two cut-off bobby pins, (have an adult help you) into each sheep for legs and insert a shorter piece into the top as a hanger.

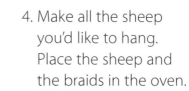

4. Make all the sheep you'd like to hang. Place the sheep and the braids in the oven.

5. After the pieces cool, paint the wreaths.

6. Paint the sheep different colors and add details with darker paint. Paint one sheep black, using white for details.

7. Glue cotton balls to the bodies of the white sheep.

8. Assemble the mobile with three ribbons. Use string to hang the white sheep from the large wreath. Suspend the black sheep from the bow at the top.

9. Now sing: "Baa baa black sheep, have you any wool? Yes sir, yes, sir, three bags full."

💡 **Use your imagination:** *To really make your mobile sing, you can write out the words to the nursery rhyme on different pieces of colored paper. Then hang them along with your sheep!*

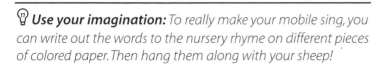

How to Make Salt Dough

1. You'll need 2 cups of flour, 1 cup of salt, and 1 cup of water.

2. Place the flour and the salt in a bowl and mix with a wooden spoon, adding water little by little until a smooth, compact dough forms. If the dough is too sticky, add a little more flour. If it's too dry, add a little water.

3. Knead the dough with your hands on a flat, very clean surface. To keep the dough from sticking, first dust the surface with a little flour.

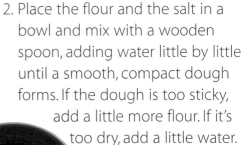

4. Once your dough figures are formed, have an adult help you place them on a baking pan and bake them in the oven at a very low temperature (about 250º) until they turn golden brown.

5. You don't need special paints to color your creations; use any non-toxic paints you have at home. You can also varnish the figures without paint or after painting them.

WHERE TO GET SUPPLIES

Art & Woodcrafters Supply, Inc.
www.artwoodcrafter.com
Order a catalog or browse online for many different craft supplies.

Craft Supplies
www.craftsfaironline.com/Supplies.html
This online craft store features many different sites, each featuring products for specific hobbies.

Darice, Inc.
21160 Drake Road
Strongsville, OH 44136-6699
www.darice.com
Order a catalog or browse online for many different craft supplies.

Making Friends
www.makingfriends.com
Offers many kits and products for children's crafts.

National Artcraft
7996 Darrow Road
Twinsburg, OH 44087
www.nationalartcraft.com
This craft store features many products available through its catalog or online.

FOR MORE INFORMATION

Books
Chapman, Gillian. *Autumn* (Seasonal Crafts). Chatham, NJ: Raintree/Steck Vaughn, 1997.
Chapman, Gillian. Pam Robson (Contributor). *Art From Fabric: With Projects Using Rags, Old Clothes, and Remnants*. New York, NY: Thomson Learning, 1995.

Connor, Nikki. Sarah Jean Neaves (Illustrator). *Cardboard Boxes* (Creating Crafts From). Providence, RI: Copper Beech Books, 1996.
Gordon, Lynn. *52 Great Art Projects For Kids*. San Francisco, CA: Chronicle Books, 1996.
King, Penny. Clare Roundhill (Contributor). *Animals* (Artists' Workshop). New York, NY: Crabtree Publishing, 1996.
Ross, Kathy. Sharon Lane Holm (Illustrator). *The Best Holiday Crafts Ever*. Brookfield, CT: Millbrook Publishing, 1996.
Smith, Alistair. *Big Book of Papercraft*. Newton, MA: Educational Development Center, 1996.

Videos
Blue's Clues Arts & Crafts. Nickelodeon. (1998).

Web Sites
Crafts For Kids
www.craftsforkids.miningco.com/mbody.htm
Many different arts and crafts activities are explained in detail.

Family Crafts
www.family.go.com
Search for crafts by age group. Projects include instructions, supply list, and helpful tips.

KinderCrafts
www.EnchantedLearning.com/Crafts
Step-by-step instructions explain how to make animal, dinosaur, box, and paper crafts, plus much more.

Making Friends
www.makingfriends.com
Contains hundreds of craft ideas with detailed instructions for children ages 2 to 12, including paper dolls, summer crafts, yucky stuff, and holiday crafts.

INDEX